VOTING Q&A

VOTING

Q&A

175+
Fascinating
Facts for
Kids

R

ROCKRIDGE
PRESS

First Rockridge Press edition 2022

Rockridge Press and the Rockridge Press logo are trademarks or registered trademarks of Callisto Media Inc. and/or its affiliates in the United States and other countries and may not be used without written permission.

For general information on our other products and services, please contact our Customer Care Department within the United States at (866) 744-2665, or outside the United States at (510) 253-0500.

Hardcover ISBN: 979-8-88608-562-4 | Paperback ISBN: 978-1-68539-456-1 | eBook ISBN: 978-1-68539-793-7

Manufactured in the United States of America

Series Designer: Diana Haas
Interior and Cover Designer: Lisa Realmuto
Art Producer: Janice Ackerman
Editor: Eliza Kirby
Production Editor: Melissa Edeburn
Production Manager: David Zapanta

Photography © Lightspring/Shutterstock, pp. Cover, ii; © Warren K. Leffler/Library of Congress, p. 3; Library of Congress, pp. 6, 60; National Photo Company Collection/Library of Congress, pp. 7, 59; © SDI Productions/iStock, pp. 10, 69–70; © Wirestock Creators/Shutterstock, p. 11; © jdross75/Shutterstock, p. 14; © ZU_09/iStock, p. 15; © Lanmas/Alamy Stock Photo, p. 18; © Luisa Ricciarini/Bridgeman Images, p. 19; © Matriyoshka/iStock, p. 22; © retrofutur/iStock, p. 23; © duncan1890/iStock, pp. 26, 32; © Universal History Archive/UIG/Bridgeman Images, pp. 27, 64; © ilbusca/iStock, p. 31; GeorgiosArt/iStock, p. 35; bauhaus1000/iStock, p. 36; © North Wind Pictures/Bridgeman Images, p. 39; © Tony Baggett/iStock, p. 40; © Keith Lance/iStock, p. 43; © Glasshouse/Alamy Stock Photo, p. 44; mj0007/iStock, p. 47; drnadig/iStock, p. 49; © Everett Collection/Shutterstock, p. 50; © Currier & Ives/Library of Congress, p. 52; © Jack Delano/Library of Congress, p. 56; © Alpha Historica/Alamy Stock Photo, p. 62; Congressional Cartography Program/Library of Congress, p. 66; © Scott J. Ferrell/Library of Congress, p. 67.

10 9 8 7 6 5 4 3 2 1 0

INTRODUCTION

Can you imagine a large group of people living without rules? There would be chaos! That's why civilizations throughout history have come up with guidelines for how people will live and function together. Different societies have used various systems of government: For example, some are led by royalty, some by dictators, and others by elected officials. Democratic societies are unique for giving citizens a say over who represents them and which laws are passed. Voting in elections is one of the most significant rights and responsibilities that members of a democracy have.

This book includes more than 175 fascinating facts about the history and evolution of voting. A glossary in the back of the book provides definitions for bolded terms, and a list of websites tells you how to find out more. This book is presented in chronological order, but you don't have to read it cover to cover. Skip around to find your favorite facts!

ELECTION ESSENTIALS

TRUE OR FALSE?

Government leaders don't have to care about what their citizens want.

FALSE.
In many civilizations throughout the past and present, citizens get to voice their opinions by voting. This type of government is called a democracy.

Q Where did the word *democracy* come from?

A It is a combination of two Greek words: *demos*, which means "people of a certain place," and *kratos*, which means "power." Together, it means "power of the people."

Q What are some modern countries that have democratic governments?

A There are lots! Examples include Australia, Canada, Finland, Norway, and the United States.

A diverse group of U.S. voters in 1962

STAT: The concept of democracy isn't new. In fact, the idea has been around for **more than 2,500 years!**

TRUE OR FALSE?

All democratic governments are the same.

FALSE.
*There are different types of democracies. There are two main categories: One is called **direct democracy** and the other one is **indirect democracy**.*

Q What is the difference between indirect and direct democracy?

A In an indirect democracy, people elect someone to represent them. That is why it can also be called a representative democracy. In a direct democracy, every citizen can vote on every law themselves.

Q Who are the representatives in an indirect democracy?

A They are individuals chosen by their peers. In the United States, for example, people vote for senators and congressmen and congresswomen to represent their interests.

Q How does a new country make a plan for their type of government?

A Usually, leaders hold meetings to discuss ideas. They create and sign official documents stating how the country will be run. In the U.S. **Constitution**, the **Founding Fathers** outlined rules about when elections would happen, who could run for office, and how citizens would be represented.

TRUE OR FALSE?

All countries today are democracies.

FALSE.

Some countries have an authoritarian government, a government in which a single ruler or political party has all the power. In authoritarian governments, citizens do not get to vote on issues or have a say in decisions, and publicly disagreeing with the leader is not allowed. Leaders can ignore existing laws because they're not accountable to the people.

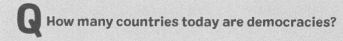

Q How many countries today are democracies?

A Some 75 modern countries are democracies, but each has a different government structure. Some of these countries are full democracies, and some are considered "flawed democracies." In these latter countries, corruption and conflict prevent people from having all the freedoms they should have.

Did You Know?

Chicago, Illinois, has a unique local government structure. Citizens are allowed to make decisions about budget issues and propose new **legislation** through the city clerk.

STAT: Switzerland, a European country with a direct democracy, currently has a population of nearly **nine million**. Swiss citizens have all the power in their government. They can even introduce legislation and call for a vote.

Did You Know?

Citizens participate in a democratic government by voting. Voting is often done with something called a ballot. A ballot is a piece of paper or other object on which people mark their choices.

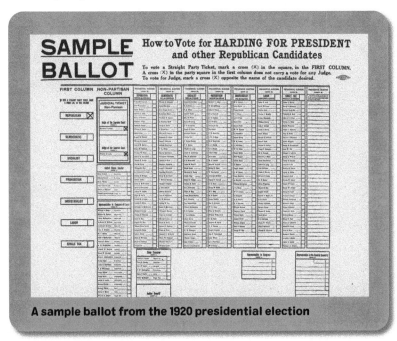

A sample ballot from the 1920 presidential election

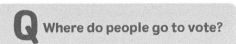

Q Where do people go to vote?

A In modern times, voting tends to occur at polling places. School gyms, churches, community centers, and supermarkets are some of the places that can serve as polling sites. There are lots of rules and security at these places to make sure votes are kept safe and secure.

Election officials counting ballots in 1924

Q Is voting still done with paper ballots?

A Not always. If voters mail in their ballots ahead of time, they use paper. When they go to a polling place, they may record their votes on a computer.

TRUE OR FALSE?

In the United States, Election Day is the same date every year.

FALSE.
Election Day doesn't always fall on the same date, but in the United States it is always the first Tuesday in November.

Did You Know?

The right to vote is called **suffrage**. People fighting for the right to vote can be called suffragists.

Q Who can vote in a democracy?

A It depends on the laws of that society. Each one is different. As time goes by, voting laws may change. When the Founding Fathers first created the U.S. government, only white men were allowed to vote. Over time, women and people of color gained the right to vote.

Q How can I become eligible to vote?

A Before voting, you need to register using official identification. You must meet the age requirements (such as being 18 or older in the United States) as well as any other conditions. For example, you usually need to be a citizen of the place where you're voting.

Q Why is voting such an important responsibility?

A In a democracy, the decisions of the government should reflect the opinions of the citizens. The best way for citizens to express their opinions is by voting for candidates and causes they agree with.

Q How often are elections held?

A In the United States, elections can be held yearly, every two years, or every four years, depending on the type of election and term. Some government positions in America and in other democratic countries may be held even longer, so elections for those are held less often.

TRUE OR FALSE?

Elections are held only when a new president or country leader is needed.

FALSE.

People vote for all types of government positions at the local, state or regional, and national level. They can also vote on new laws.

Q What are some examples of things people in the United States may vote for at these different levels?

A At the local level, voters may elect candidates to fill offices such as a mayor or sheriff. They may vote *yes* or *no* on sales tax. At a state level, voters elect offices like the governor or lieutenant governor. At the national level, voters cast their votes for the president, vice president, and members of Congress.

Q What happens to candidates who lose their elections?

A Most elections can have only one winner. Sometimes, the runners-up will aid and advise the winner who takes office. For example, in the early days of the United States, the role of vice president was filled by whoever came in second place in the presidential election. Some candidates who don't win their elections will go on to do something else entirely. Others who don't win the first time will run again for another role in government.

STAT: Harold E. Stassen, former governor of Minnesota, ran for president of the United States **nine** different times! (He never won.)

A citizen casting a ballot

VOTING LONG AGO

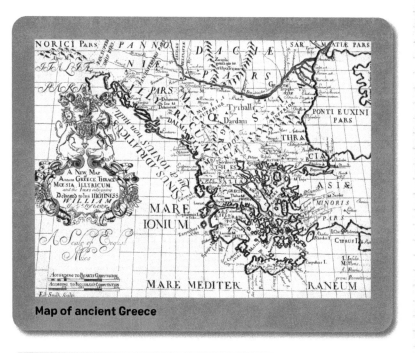

Map of ancient Greece

Q Where was the first democracy?

A Historians believe that ancient Greece is the oldest instance of a democracy.

Q About how long ago was the idea of democracy created in ancient Greece?

A The civilization was first formed in 500 BCE. That means democracy has been around for more than 2,500 years!

Did You Know?

Greece is a country in Europe. Modern-day Greece is located in a concentrated area near the Mediterranean Sea. Ancient Greece was more spread out.

 Q Was ancient Greece just one big country?

A No, it was divided into city-states, something like the 50 states that make up the United States. Each city-state in ancient Greece did things their own way. Here are some examples:

NAME OF CITY-STATE	FORM OF GOVERNMENT
Athens	Democratic beliefs
Sparta	Ruled by two kings and a council of elders
Ithaca	Democratic beliefs
Corinth	Ruled by high-class "noblemen"
Mycenae	Ruled by a king

TRUE OR FALSE?

Sparta was where democracy started.

FALSE.

It was Athens. The city-state of Sparta was focused on building strong warriors. Developing a powerful military was the most important thing in Sparta.

TRUE OR FALSE?

Democracy in ancient Greece was the same as it is in the United States today.

FALSE.

Government has definitely evolved over the past 2,500+ years. Many things are different now. Just one example is the way that voting is done. The ancient Greeks could never have imagined digital voting machines! Another big difference is how many more people have the right to vote today than in ancient Greece.

Q What kind of a democracy did they have in ancient Greece?

A Athens had a direct democracy. That means that citizens cast their votes themselves instead of picking a representative. One issue they would vote on was whether or not to go to war.

Q Who came up with the idea for a democratic government?

A The man who is credited with helping organize Athens into a democracy was named Pericles. He based his ideas on the thoughts of some previous thinkers named Protagoras, Zeno, and Anaxagoras.

Q If you go to Greece now, can you see any buildings from the ancient civilization?

A Yes! Athens was built up on a hill in an area called the Acropolis. Voting was done in a hillside auditorium close by. Some of the buildings and structures are now in ruins, but others are still in one piece. For example, you can see a building called the Parthenon. (Pericles came up with the idea for that, too.) It's a great example of the type of architecture used in ancient Greece for buildings where voting and government functions took place.

Did You Know?

There is a replica of the Parthenon in Nashville, Tennessee. You can plan a visit to see an exact copy of the 2,500-year-old building in Athens!

Replica of the Parthenon in Nashville, Tennessee

Q Did anyone in ancient Greece oppose the idea of democracy?

A Yes. For example, one of Greece's most influential philosophers, Socrates, didn't believe in democracy. Socrates believed that having one strong ruler was better than a democracy because people may not be well-informed enough on issues to vote on them. Some of his philosophies later inspired Benjamin Franklin, Martin Luther King Jr., and other great thinkers.

Q Was there a king in ancient Greece?

A For hundreds of years, ancient Greece was ruled by kings. But once the idea of a democratic government came about, there was no longer just one person in charge. That's because a democracy is for the people, by the people!

Sokrates.

Socrates

TRUE OR FALSE?

Everyone in ancient Greece could vote.

FALSE.
Only people considered citizens could vote.

Q Who was considered a citizen?

A Men who were not enslaved were considered citizens. Women, children, and enslaved men were not.

STAT: About **40,000** men could vote in ancient Greece. This number was only about 10 percent of the total population!

Q What kind of leaders did ancient Greece have?

A 500 voters were randomly selected to make up a governing body called a council.

Q Did these citizens who were randomly selected have to participate?

A Yes. If you didn't, your hand might be painted red so everyone would know you didn't participate.

Q What types of things did the council of 500 citizens do?

A The council had to serve for one year. They would pass new laws and organize elections.

Q How often did the council of 500 meet?

A The council, also called the boule, met every day!

Q What was it called when the citizens met to vote?

A The meetings for an election were called assemblies. The Greek name was *ekklesia*. Historians think only about 5,000 voters would typically attend. Men who didn't attend were likely part of the army or navy or working other jobs.

Q What type of things might members of the assembly, or *ekklesia*, have voted on?

A They would not be voting for government leaders, because the 500 members of the council were chosen randomly. Instead, they voted on what their relationships with other city-states should be and when to go to war.

TRUE OR FALSE?

People had to show up in person to vote.

TRUE.

In a direct democracy like ancient Greece's, you had to show up to give your vote.

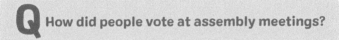

Q How did people vote at assembly meetings?

A Sometimes they would just raise their hand to vote and say "yea" for yes or "nay" for no. Other times they would cast a physical ballot.

A stone relief depicting ancient Greek voters

Did You Know?

In ancient Greece, paper hadn't been invented yet. Citizens cast their votes on broken pieces of pottery.

 Q What were these pieces called?

A The broken pieces of pottery were called ostraca.

Broken pottery pieces used for voting

Did You Know?

The word *ostracized* comes from ostraca. Ostracized means to be left out. Sometimes citizens would write the name of a person they wanted banished from Athens. If enough people voted against that person, they would be kicked out!

STAT: In the 1960s, archaeologists found a type of garbage dump in the ruins of ancient Greece. They discovered **9,000** ostraca with names etched onto them!

Q How did the ancient Greeks write their votes?

A They didn't have pencils or pens, so voters scratched on the pieces of ostraca. They used the Greek alphabet, which had its own set of symbols, though a few of them resemble letters that we use today. You can find examples of the Greek alphabet in use today for the names of college fraternities and sororities!

Did You Know?

An important part of the government in ancient Greece was the court system, called the *dikasteria*. Athens had no police, so citizens could bring cases to court themselves. Sometimes they would bring cases just because they were mad at someone and wanted to humiliate them!

Q Are the ancient Greeks known only for creating democracy?

A No, the ancient Greeks had a huge influence on many aspects of society. They were known for their emphasis on arts, culture, and philosophy. They are also credited with creating the Olympics!

Q Was the city-state of Sparta a democracy, too?

A No, it was an **oligarchy**, which means only a few people had power. Two kings who inherited the throne because they were born into a royal family were in charge, along with a council of 28 elders. The elders had to be over age 60 and come from rich families. There was some voting, but it was done only by rich and powerful citizens. The military was the most important thing to Sparta.

Q How did democracy start spreading outside of Athens?

A Alexander the Great was the king of a part of Greece called Macedonia. He wanted to build a huge empire. He conquered other places and spread the idea of democracy to the places he took over, starting a few years after 330 BCE.

Q Why was he called Alexander the Great?

A Because he was such a powerful leader with strong military strategies. After he died in 323 BCE, his influence lived on in the places he conquered. More people started learning to speak Greek and sharing Greek values.

Q What were some of the places Alexander the Great conquered?

A He conquered Persia, Phoenicia, Israel, and Egypt. Phoenicia is where modern-day Syria, Lebanon, and north Israel are. Persia is the current location of Iran.

Q Did democracy and the idea of voting spread to ancient Egypt?

A Not exactly, but after Alexander the Great died, his general Ptolemy created a government that put power into the hands of many officials, not just a king. The new government lasted for a couple hundred years. Then Egypt went back to being a **theocracy**, which is a government ruled by a religious figure.

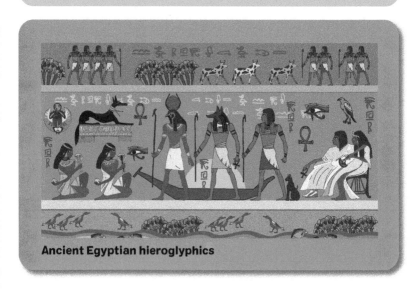

Ancient Egyptian hieroglyphics

Q Did democracy spread to any other nearby civilizations?

A Yes! One example is ancient Rome. Its king was overthrown around 509 BCE. Exciting changes in arts, science, and technology created demand for a more modern type of government. People started viewing the world differently thanks to evolving philosophies. Inspired by ancient Greece, Rome became a **republic**, a type of government in which citizens elect representatives.

Q Did all citizens in ancient Rome vote?

A No, only free men could vote. They elected senators and wrote down laws on tablets.

STAT: Historians think that around **one million** people lived in the city of Rome when it was most crowded. Only about **150,000** people lived in Athens at that same time.

A Roman soldier

TRUE OR FALSE?

Ancient India did not have a democratic government.

FALSE.

Thanks to Greek influence, people in ancient India did develop a type of democracy around 400 BCE. People lived in villages at the time. Adult men would meet in an assembly to make decisions for their village.

Myth:

The idea of voting spread to civilizations everywhere in the world.

Fact:

Democracy did not catch on in the ancient world outside of Europe and the Middle East. About 1,500 years after the fall of the Greek Empire, the Aztec civilization (in what is now Mexico) used a system in which noblemen elected advisors to the emperor. But the emperor himself was still all-powerful and was believed to represent the gods' will on earth.

Q **What is the Aztec civilization known for?**

A The Aztecs are known for building impressive temples for worship and for making new developments in farming. They also had strong warriors and a powerful leader called an emperor who made all decisions.

MONARCHS IN EUROPE

Myth:

Historians consider the period after the ancient Roman Empire to be the Dark Ages.

Fact:

There were a lot of important changes in arts, culture, and forms of government during this era. Experts feel that calling it the "Dark Ages" is unfair. The preferred term is the Early Middle Ages, and the period lasted from about 500 CE to the late 1400s CE.

Q What economic system was in use during the Middle Ages?

A Most of Europe during the Middle Ages operated under the economic system of **feudalism**. Here's how it worked: A king gave farmland called "fiefs" to powerful men. Citizens without land, called "serfs," would work the land in exchange for a place to live.

Q What changes did feudalism bring to Europe?

A It led to new farming techniques, which meant that crops could grow more quickly. And that meant fewer people were needed to work the land. The landowners also started to demand more of a say in how the king did things.

A knight pledging his service to a lord

Did You Know?

Most governments in Medieval Europe were **absolute monarchies**. One ruler made all the laws and decisions. Many of them ruled for long periods of time.

Q What were some advantages and disadvantages of absolute monarchies?

A A clear disadvantage was that unless you were the king, your opinion really didn't matter! This started to frustrate a lot of people. An advantage of monarchies, though, was protection. The king's job was to keep his subjects safe, and he took that very seriously.

Myth:

If you were a king during the Middle Ages, you could do whatever you wanted.

Fact:

That was definitely not true in the year 1215. Powerful men in England got so tired of King John's cruel behavior that they made him sign a document called the Magna Carta, which limited his own power. Some of the ideals in that charter are included in the Declaration of Independence and U.S. Constitution.

King John being forced to sign the Magna Carta

Myth:

The Magna Carta was written in English.

Fact:

It was actually written in Latin, which was a written language but not a spoken one. The name Magna Carta means "great charter."

TRUE OR FALSE?

There was only one version of the Magna Carta.

FALSE.

Changes were made in 1216, 1217, and 1225. The updates helped guarantee that the king didn't have too much power and established fair ways to have trials.

Q Have any copies of the Magna Carta ever been outside of England?

A Yes! One was on display at the 1939 World's Fair in New York City. When the fair ended, it was too dangerous to ship the copy back to England due to the outbreak of World War II. The Magna Carta was stored safely with some other important historical documents in Ft. Knox, Kentucky, until the war was over. Afterward, it was returned to England.

Q Can you see a copy of the Magna Carta today?

A Yes, but you need to pack a suitcase for the United Kingdom! There are two copies in different cathedrals in England and two copies in the British Library.

STAT: There were 63 different clauses that were part of the original Magna Carta. Those sections benefitted wealthy landowners greatly!

Q Did any places in Europe have elections during the Middle Ages?

A Yes. One example is the city of Venice, Italy. Around the 1300s, citizens established a governing body called a Great Council. Members of powerful families made up the council. It had 40 members; each one would cast their vote for candidates they liked and no votes for candidates they didn't. This system, called "approval voting," led to a winner with the most votes. These people they elected made up a senate with 200 to 300 members.

Did You Know?

The senate in medieval Venice selected 10 of its members to have control. One member of this secret group was selected to be the doge, or head of the city, but in name only. The doge had no more power than the rest of the group of 10.

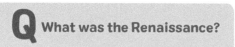

Q What led to the end of the Middle Ages?

A Around the 1400s, there was a shift in Europe. A widespread famine, the 100 Years' War, and the Black Plague led to suffering and death. People started looking at their lives differently. They developed an interest in ancient Greek culture, which led to new developments in the arts and science. Perhaps the biggest change came from the Crusades, which were religious wars designed to spread Christianity. They led to exploration of other areas, which brought Europe into the Global Age.

TRUE OR FALSE?

The Global Age was when Europeans first began exploring continents all across the globe.

TRUE.

The word global *means around the world. The Global Age lasted from the late 1400s until the mid 1700s. People started exploring more of the globe through trade and other interaction with civilizations in different countries and even on different continents.*

Q What was the Renaissance?

A It was a time period spanning the 1400s and 1500s and continuing into the 1600s. *Renaissance* is a French word that means "rebirth," and the time period's name refers to the rebirth of art, science, culture, and philosophy.

Q What was the printing press and why was its invention significant?

A The printing press was a machine modernized by Johannes Gutenberg. It is thought to have been originally developed in China. Gutenberg combined metals like molten lead and brass to make a machine that was able to take ink and print words. Before this, people called scribes would handwrite everything! Thanks to the printing press, more people were able to read—which meant more members of the public knew and had opinions about what was going on in government.

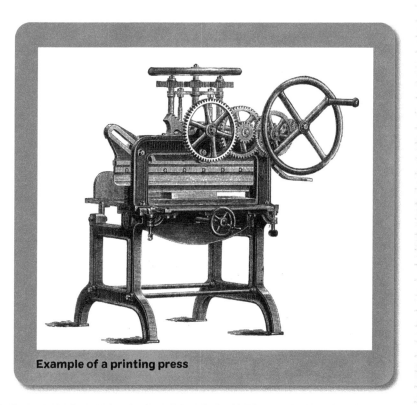

Example of a printing press

What kinds of changes were happening in governments during the Renaissance?

A Religion and government started joining forces. This led to monarchs having total control over religious beliefs and power. For example, when King Henry VIII of England got frustrated that the Catholic church wouldn't allow him to get a divorce, he made Parliament pass a law putting him in control of the Church of England. That way *he* could make the rules!

TRUE OR FALSE?

There were still monarchs during the Renaissance.

TRUE.

There were definitely still monarchs, and they had more power than ever.

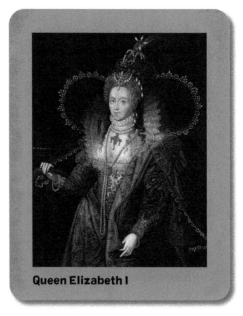

Queen Elizabeth I

Q Who were some of the absolute monarchs in England during the late Middle Ages and Renaissance?

A Henry VIII, who took control of the Church of England in the 1500s so he could do things his way, was one example. A decade after his death, Elizabeth I took over as queen of England and Ireland. Unusually for a female monarch, she refused to get married and felt strongly about being a powerful leader in her own right.

STAT: Louis XIV, who was nicknamed the "Sun King," was the ruler of France for **72 years**. This is the longest reign of any monarch in history!

Q What was the Enlightenment?

A To be *enlightened* means to have learned more and have a better understanding. The period between the 1600s and 1800s is called the Enlightenment because there were many scientific discoveries and new inventions during this time. People were losing patience with the absolute monarchs and thought that the government should not have so much power.

Q What is a **parliamentary government**?

A It's a government in which a group of official leaders gets a say in making laws—not just the monarch. This helps create a balance of power.

Q How did the English monarch's power come to be limited?

A A 1611 legal decision called the Case of Proclamations declared that monarchs could no longer make certain choices without consulting Parliament, England's **legislative branch**. England had first established its Parliament 400 years earlier, but now it was claiming more power.

Q How did the English Parliament use its new power?

A In 1628, Parliament sent a document called the Petition of Right to King Charles I. In it, Parliament declared that the taxes Charles was charging to fund a war with Spain were unfair. The legislators felt that these taxes went against the Magna Carta, which stated that monarchs could not impose taxes without consent. In the Petition of Right, Parliament also stated that the king could not imprison people without a reason. All of this made the king more accountable to Parliament.

King Charles I

Myth:
The idea of "no taxation without representation" was created by Americans during the Revolutionary War.

Fact:
This term was commonly used in the years after the Petition of Right, when Parliament thought King Charles I was charging taxes for selfish reasons.

Q What is something King Charles I did that Parliament disagreed with?

A He was forcing the people under his rule to give him money as a "gift." It wasn't a gift because he was making them give it. If they didn't obey, he would put them in jail!

Did You Know?

There were political parties of sorts as early as 1678 in England. People who supported the king and the Church of England were called Whigs, and people who didn't were called Tories.

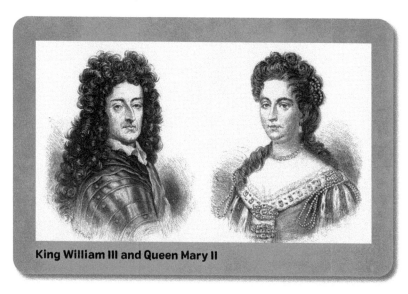

King William III and Queen Mary II

Q Were there other documents or laws that created political change in England during the 1600s?

A Yes. The English Bill of Rights, which was signed by rulers William III and Mary II in 1689, changed everything for government structure in England. It gave Parliament more decision-making power than the monarch. It was a type of constitution, a written plan for how a government would be organized. Since 1689, England's government has been a **constitutional monarchy**.

Q Did anyone during the Enlightenment think that ordinary people—not just the king and members of Parliament—should have rights?

A Absolutely. One important philosopher who believed that the rights of the people should be considered was John Locke. His ideas played an important role in the English Bill of Rights.

TRUE OR FALSE?

Jean-Jacques Rousseau was a French king.

FALSE.
Rousseau was a philosopher born in Switzerland, though he did live much of his life in France. He is known for having strong opinions about politics. He believed in limiting governmental power and giving individuals more rights.

Q Did John Locke and Jean-Jacques Rousseau know each other?

A Although they had similar philosophies, they never met. Locke passed away in 1704 and Rousseau wasn't born until 1712.

VOTING IN THE NEW WORLD

Q Why were the Americas called the "New World"?

A Because they were new to the Europeans! North, South, and Central America had been home to thriving civilizations for thousands of years, but Europeans weren't aware of them until the 1400s.

Q What made Europeans want to start settling in the New World?

A Some Europeans moved to America because they didn't like how much power the monarchy had. For example, the king of England felt everyone should practice the same religion, and some people had different beliefs. One such group of people were called the Pilgrims. In 1620, 100 of them departed England and sailed a ship called the *Mayflower* to what is now Massachusetts.

Q Did the Pilgrims establish a form of government?

A Yes! They formed a government before even leaving the ship. 41 men signed a document called the Mayflower Compact. It created laws and decided how voting would be done.

Did You Know?

The Mayflower Compact established that all men over age 21 would vote in person in the Plymouth **Colony**. On November 21, 1620, they elected John Carver as the first governor.

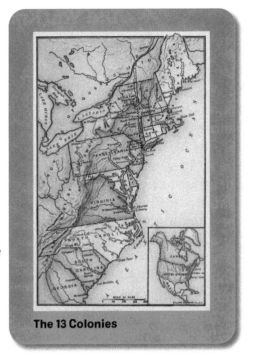

The 13 Colonies

Q Did all the colonists stay in Plymouth?

A No—if they had, we wouldn't have 50 states today! English settlers spread up north and down south along the east coast of America.

STAT: There were **13** colonies divided into three regions based on their location along the Atlantic coast. The regions were the New England Colonies, the Middle Colonies, and the Southern Colonies.

Did You Know?

Freedom of religion was really important to William Penn, the founder of Pennsylvania Colony. He created a "Frame of Government," the first written document outlining a system of government that included a way for **amendments** to be made later. Penn recognized that society, and therefore the needs for government, could change over time.

William Penn

Q Were British colonists the only European settlers in the New World?

A No. The French had also been exploring the colonies, and they had developed a good relationship with the Native Americans. Disagreements started when both England and France tried to claim the same territory as their own. Some of the Native American nations sided with the French, and some sided with the British. This led to a conflict called the Seven Years' War, also known as the French and Indian War.

Q What was the impact of the Seven Years' War?

A The war, which lasted from 1756 to 1763, resulted in a victory for the British—but it came at a cost. They made an enemy of the French. They also were in major debt after borrowing money to pay soldiers.

Myth:

The Founding Fathers were not involved in the Seven Years' War.

Fact:

A 22-year-old George Washington fought for England during the war. He made many mistakes in battle, which helped him be a better soldier later on.

Q How did life in the colonies change after the Seven Years' War?

A King George III decided to station some British soldiers in the colonies to prevent future conflict. This extra expense put him in even more debt. He decided to raise money by creating new taxes.

TRUE OR FALSE?

The Stamp Act was a tax on postage stamps.

FALSE.

A mail system as we know it didn't exist yet. The Stamp Act, passed by Parliament in 1765, was the king's way of taxing all paper items in the colonies, including letters, newspapers, and even playing cards!

Q What was the Tea Act?

A The king tried to force colonists to buy tea exclusively from the East India Company. That way, he could impose taxes on the tea, and he could charge whatever he wanted. This unpopular rule led directly to the Boston Tea Party. A band of patriots in a secret group called the Sons of Liberty dumped tea into Boston Harbor in protest.

Q What else did the British government do to make life hard for the American colonists?

A They passed several acts in 1774 which together became known as the Intolerable Acts. These included a law that closed Boston Harbor, another that allowed the British soldiers to take over buildings, and more. Life under British rule was getting harder and harder for the colonists to bear.

Q How did the colonists feel about the changes happening by the 1760s and 1770s?

A They were frustrated! They felt it wasn't fair that the king was all the way across the Atlantic Ocean, making decisions for them and charging them taxes without caring about their needs. They started to plan a way to make things different in the colonies.

Q What was the Continental Congress?

A It was a formal organization of Founding Fathers who met to discuss their issues with the king and to find ways to express their frustrations with the taxes. The first Continental Congress session, which began in September 1774, included 56 representatives from most of the colonies.

Q Who was Thomas Paine?

A Thomas Paine tried many career paths in England and wasn't successful. Once he moved to the colonies in 1774, he found success with writing and journalism. In 1776, he published a pamphlet called *Common Sense*. He expressed his conviction that the colonists should try to break away from the king.

Thomas Paine

Q When did the colonists decide to officially take a stand against King George III?

A After Thomas Paine published *Common Sense*, the colonists realized the need to form their own country, separate from England. In 1776, a committee of five men met to write the Declaration of Independence. This group included Founding Fathers John Adams, Benjamin Franklin, and Thomas Jefferson.

Thomas Jefferson drafting the Declaration of Independence with input from other Founding Fathers

Myth:

Thomas Jefferson wrote the Declaration of Independence alone.

Fact:

Other committee members helped him. He was also motivated by the ideas of Enlightenment-era philosopher John Locke. Locke is known for his philosophy that all men are entitled to life, liberty, and property. For the Declaration of Independence, Jefferson changed "property" to "the pursuit of happiness."

STAT: After Congress voted to approve it, **200** unsigned copies of the Declaration of Independence were printed and given out.

Did You Know?

Some of the colonists, called loyalists, disagreed with declaring independence. Those who felt that the colonists should lead their own country were called patriots.

Q What was the American Revolution?

A This was the war immediately following the Declaration of Independence. King George III was not happy that the colonists were demanding freedom. He sent even more soldiers to keep the colonists in line. After many battles, the colonists achieved victory. In 1783, the war was declared over, and the Treaty of Paris was signed. The colonists would govern their own country at last.

Did You Know?

Some of the colonies, like Virginia, had their own constitutions before there was an official United States Constitution.

Q What were the Articles of Confederation?

A The Articles of Confederation created a plan to organize the new American government. They were adopted November 15, 1777, during the American Revolution, but they didn't last because they didn't establish a national leader or a military for protection. The Articles of Confederation were replaced by the United States Constitution in 1787.

Q How was the United States Constitution created?

A In 1787, representatives from the 13 original states met in Pennsylvania for the Constitutional Convention, a meeting to replace the Articles of Confederation. The Constitution would establish the law of the land, who would lead the new country, how those leaders would be elected, how much power they would have, how their authority would be enforced, and more.

Q Who was in charge of writing the Constitution?

A James Madison is considered the "Father of the Constitution" because he did most of the writing. He included the idea of **checks and balances** by establishing an **executive branch**, a **legislative branch**, and a **judicial branch**. That way no one branch of government would have too much power.

The first lines of the Constitution

TRUE OR FALSE?

The United States Constitution was the first written constitution for any country in history.

TRUE.
Many other countries would later follow suit.

Q What was federalism?

A Federalism was the idea that the newly formed United States should function as one **sovereign**, or central, government while also giving some limited powers to the individual states. An entire political party, called the Federalist party, was formed based on this belief. To try to convince people of the value of federalism, a series of influential essays called *The Federalist Papers* was published from late 1787 to early 1788.

Q What were other early political parties?

A The other major party, led by Thomas Jefferson, was the Republican party. Unlike Federalists, Republicans felt that states should have more rights, the national government's power should be limited, and there should not be a national bank.

Q Why did the U.S. Constitution include both a House of Representatives and a Senate?

A Delegates from smaller states were concerned they wouldn't have much of a say if the number of representatives was directly proportional to population. The solution came in the form of a two-part legislative branch. Every state would have two members in the Senate no matter how big or small it was. The number of representatives in the House of Representatives, on the other hand, would be based on the population of each state.

Did You Know?

Benjamin Franklin played an integral role in the creation of the U.S. Constitution despite being in his 80s—more than twice as old as Thomas Jefferson, and 50 years older than Alexander Hamilton!

Q What did the Constitution establish about electing a president?

A It set a president's term as four years long—unlike the British king, who was ruler for life. It also determined that the president would be commander in chief of the militia. It established how the Electoral College would work and stated that only white men who owned land could vote in elections.

Myth:

The Founding Fathers didn't discuss enslaved people at the Constitutional Convention.

Fact:

Most of the signers of the Declaration of Independence were enslavers themselves. They knew that having liberty for all in the Constitution went against this, but they did not want to give up their unpaid laborers. After much debate, they ultimately decided to include clauses that addressed enslavement in a general way that could be left to interpretation.

The U.S. Capitol building, where Congress meets today

Q What was the first presidential election like?

A Each state chose people to be electors, and only they got to vote. The electors chose George Washington to be president. John Adams became vice president because he received the second-most votes.

Q Did George Washington want to run for a second presidential term?

A No. At 60, he felt that he was too old. But he wanted to keep the peace between Federalists and Republicans, so he ran again. He had no opponent in the 1792 election, so he won and served a second term.

George Washington

Q Could changes be made to the Constitution?

A Yes. The Founding Fathers knew that the original Constitution was not perfect. During the Constitutional Convention, the delegates agreed that more specific rights could be added later.

Did You Know?

In 1789, about two years after the initial U.S. Constitution was adopted, the first 10 amendments were added. Collectively, these amendments are called the Bill of Rights.

THE BILL OF RIGHTS

AMENDMENT NUMBER	WHAT RIGHT IT INVOLVES
1st Amendment	Freedom of speech, religion, the press, right to petition
2nd Amendment	Right to bear arms and form a militia
3rd Amendment	No quartering soldiers without the homeowner's consent
4th Amendment	No search and seizure without a warrant
5th Amendment	You don't have to testify against yourself
6th Amendment	Right to a speedy trial
7th Amendment	Right to a jury trial of peers
8th Amendment	No cruel and unusual punishment
9th Amendment	People have other rights that aren't spelled out here
10th Amendment	States have rights

FIGHTING FOR VOTES

Q Were the American colonists the only people who declared freedom from monarchy in the 1700s?

A Not at all. The French Revolution began in 1789 with the Declaration of the Rights of Man and the Citizen, which had 17 articles detailing freedoms that the French people were entitled to.

Q What was the result of the French Revolution?

A After the revolution, France's government was no longer a monarchy, women had more rights, and enslavement was **abolished**.

French Revolutionaries destroying royal property

TRUE OR FALSE?

Haiti became a republic shortly after the United States won its independence from England.

TRUE.

The country of Haiti became a republic in 1804 after going through its own revolution. Haiti shares an island with the Dominican Republic and is about 700 miles southeast of Florida.

Q Which country had control of Haiti at the time of its revolution in 1804?

A The Spanish were the first Europeans to settle Haiti, around the time when Christopher Columbus arrived in America. Spanish explorers were searching for gold there. They treated **Indigenous** people unfairly, and many of the Indigenous people died after being exposed to diseases by Europeans. The French took over by the mid-1600s and were in control of the country when it rebelled against colonial rule in 1804.

STAT: At the time of the Haitian Revolution, the population of Haiti was around **556,000**. **500,000** were enslaved Africans.

Did You Know?

Haiti was the first country in the world to be founded by formerly enslaved people.

Q Were there other revolutions in the 1800s?

A Yes, there were several uprisings throughout Europe in 1848. The modern-day countries of Austria, Denmark, France, Italy, and the Netherlands were just a few that were involved. In most cases, citizens rebelled because they were frustrated that monarchies had too much power.

TRUE OR FALSE?

The revolutions of 1848 started in Italy.

TRUE.

In January 1848, a small conflict began on the island of Sicily. The next phase followed in France a month later and then continued to spread throughout Europe.

Q Did the revolutions of 1848 create real change in any countries that were involved?

A Yes, serfdom ended in Austria. Serfs were lower-class citizens who had few rights and were required to be at the service of a higher-class lord. Also, Denmark's absolute monarchy came to an end after hundreds of years. The government structure for the Netherlands changed as well. After the revolutions of 1848, the country instituted a representative democracy.

Did You Know?

There were three amendments to the U.S. Constitution passed in 1865, immediately following the Civil War. These were referred to as the **Reconstruction** Amendments.

Q What rights did the Reconstruction Amendments establish?

A The 13th Amendment, **ratified** December 6, 1865, officially abolished slavery in the United States. The 14th Amendment, which was ratified July 9, 1868, granted all the rights previously established in the U.S. Constitution to formerly enslaved citizens. The final Reconstruction Amendment was the 15th Amendment. It was ratified February 3, 1870, and made it clear that previously enslaved men had the right to vote.

Q How did white Southerners try to prevent newly freed African Americans from voting?

A They threatened violence and formed a terrorist group called the Ku Klux Klan (or KKK) to scare people so they wouldn't even register to vote. They also required voters to take a literacy test to register. The tests were challenging and unfair because enslaved people were forbidden from learning how to read. Another tactic was to charge a poll tax, which most of the freed men could not afford.

Q What were "Jim Crow" laws?

A Jim Crow laws limited the rights of previously enslaved citizens. The laws, at local and state levels, created a path for **segregation** in lots of public places.

A segregated bus station in Durham, North Carolina, in 1940

Did You Know?

The first African American man elected to Congress was named Hiram Rhodes Revels. He was a Mississippi native who took his seat in 1870.

Q Who was the first African American state governor?

A Technically, it was Pinckney Benton Stewart Pinchback in 1872. Pinchback had become the lieutenant governor of Louisiana after the previous lieutenant governor died. When the governor was removed from office, Pinchback took over. The first African American man *elected* governor was Douglas Wilder of Virginia in 1990.

TRUE OR FALSE?

After the 15th Amendment, all citizens in the United States over 18 had the right to vote.

FALSE.
Only men over the age of 21 had the right to vote at this time.

Q What ignited the women's suffrage movement?

A A convention held in Seneca Falls, New York, in July 1848 was the spark that started the movement. Two women's rights activists, Lucretia Mott and Elizabeth Cady Stanton, had been forbidden from attending an event in London simply because they were women. They decided to just have their own gathering in New York!

Q Who was Susan B. Anthony?

A After meeting Elizabeth Cady Stanton, Susan B. Anthony became a powerful agent for change. She wrote newspaper articles, gave speeches, and lobbied Congress to give women the right to vote. She faced a lot of adversity because many people disagreed with her. She even had to pay a fine for trying to vote.

Q What were some of the challenges faced by suffragists?

A Women faced discrimination from a lot of men who didn't think they should have a voice in politics. Most women at the time didn't attend college, so they weren't as educated and informed about issues. They also didn't work outside the home or own property. African American women faced even more challenges than white women.

Q Who was Ida B. Wells?

A Ida B. Wells was a journalist who brought to light many issues involving inequality. As an African American woman, Wells faced all kinds of prejudice. She spoke out about the additional challenges African American suffragists faced.

Q How did suffragists spread the word about their cause?

A They held conventions and parades, formed organizations, and wrote letters. Women lobbied government officials and gave speeches. They wrote their own "Declaration of Sentiments," which was inspired by the Declaration of Independence.

Q When did women get the right to vote?

A After many years of fighting, suffragists finally achieved victory with the passage of the 19th Amendment. When it was ratified in 1920, women got the right to vote.

Women sewing stars on a flag each time a new state approved the 19th Amendment

Congresswoman Jeannette Rankin

Myth:

No women were elected to serve in the United States government until after the 19th Amendment was passed.

Fact:

Congresswoman Jeannette Rankin of Montana became the first female member of Congress after she was elected in 1916. She was the only member of Congress to later oppose the U.S. entering World War I and World War II.

STAT: When the 19th Amendment was passed, an estimated **26 million** women over the age of 21 became eligible to vote.

Did You Know?

Harriet Tubman, who led enslaved people to freedom on the Underground Railroad, was later an important member of the women's suffrage movement.

Did You Know?

In 1924, Nellie Tayloe Ross was elected governor of Wyoming—the first woman to be governor in any U.S. state. She later served as the Democratic National Committee vice chairman and director of the U.S. Mint, which makes coins.

Q What social justice changes were happening in the United States in the 1960s?

A The **Civil Rights** Movement began picking up steam in the 1960s. More people began speaking out against unfair treatment of African Americans. Landmark court cases overturned segregation in schools. As more households bought television sets, more and more Americans could see discrimination on the news.

Q What was Lyndon B. Johnson's role in the Civil Rights Movement?

A Johnson became president after John F. Kennedy was assassinated in 1963. Both Johnson and Kennedy were passionate about civil rights issues. Johnson signed several important pieces of legislation granting more rights to African Americans.

President Lyndon B. Johnson meeting with Martin Luther King Jr. and other civil rights leaders

Q What was the March on Washington?

A It was a gathering of 200,000 people near the Lincoln Memorial on August 28, 1963. Participants of diverse backgrounds came from across the United States to Washington, D.C., to show support for civil rights legislation and voting equality. This was where Martin Luther King Jr. gave his famous "I Have a Dream" speech. A young future Congressman John Lewis also shared powerful words that inspired the crowd.

Q What was the Civil Rights Act of 1964?

A The Civil Rights Act was a piece of legislation started by John F. Kennedy and signed into law by Lyndon B. Johnson. It ended segregation in places like public restrooms, restaurants, and buses. It also created policies for equal treatment in the workplace. This act paved the way for voting rights to be addressed.

Q What was "Freedom Summer"?

A "Freedom Summer" was the nickname for the summer of 1964, after the signing of the Civil Rights Act. Hundreds of white volunteers joined the voting rights cause. Their plan was to travel to the most segregated parts of the South, like Mississippi, and register African American voters. But violence prevented participants from reaching as many voters as they wanted to. This helped Lyndon B. Johnson see the need for more federal legislation to ensure voting equality.

Q Were any amendments protecting voting rights added to the Constitution?

A Yes, the 24th Amendment eliminated poll taxes. It was ratified on January 23, 1964. Voters would no longer be denied the right to vote due to inability to pay a tax.

Did You Know?

The Voting Rights Act was signed into law by Lyndon B. Johnson in 1965. It put an end to many common practices, such as literacy tests, that had limited African Americans' voting rights.

Lyndon B. Johnson

Did You Know?

The state of South Carolina challenged part of the new Voting Rights Act in 1966, in a case known as *South Carolina v. Katzenbach* that went all the way to the Supreme Court. The Supreme Court ruled that the Voting Rights Act was backed up by the 15th Amendment, and the state of South Carolina lost.

VOTING TODAY

TRUE OR FALSE?

Eighteen is the minimum voting age everywhere.

FALSE.
In some countries, including Argentina, Brazil, and Scotland, you can vote when you're only 16. In a few African countries, citizens must be 21 or older to vote.

> **Q** When did the voting age in the United States become 18?

> **A** The 26th Amendment, ratified in 1971, lowered the voting age to 18. One deciding factor was the fact that citizens this age could serve in the military.

TRUE OR FALSE?

The 25th Amendment gave people living in Washington, D.C., the right to vote for electors.

FALSE.
It was the 23rd Amendment, passed in 1961. This was necessary because Washington, D.C., isn't part of a state, so its residents didn't technically have a way to vote for the president. Now they have a say by choosing members of the Electoral College to represent them.

Myth:

Whichever candidate receives the most votes across the country becomes the next president.

Fact:

The Electoral College, which has been in place since America's founding, means that the **popular vote** isn't how the presidency is won. The Electoral College was a system created to ensure that states with smaller populations would still have a meaningful say in national elections.

Did You Know?

A presidential candidate has won the popular vote but not the Electoral College vote five times.

STAT: The state with the most electoral votes is California, with 55 total. The state population is more than **39 million** people.

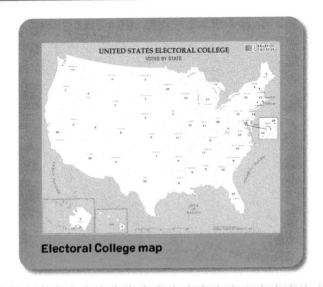

Electoral College map

Q How often are presidential elections held?

A Presidential elections are held every four years. Candidates first have to be chosen through primary elections held by major political parties. Then the real campaigns begin. The candidates who were chosen in the primaries give speeches, make commercials and signs, and meet with voters.

A politician greeting voters at a rally

Q Can the same person keep being elected president over and over?

A No. The 22nd Amendment established a limit of two presidential terms. It was passed by Congress in 1947 and ratified in 1951, after President Franklin D. Roosevelt had been elected four times. Americans wanted to limit presidential terms so that the government didn't start to feel like a monarchy.

Q What happens if the president dies while in office?

A The 25th Amendment says that the vice president takes over.

Q What are some changes that have been made to ballots in the United States over time?

A Believe it or not, voting was first done by standing in line and saying your vote out loud. There was no privacy. Then votes were done on random scraps of paper! Things started to get more official with the use of tickets, which resembled train tickets, in the mid-1800s.

Q When did a machine start to be used for voting in the United States?

A An inventor named Jacob H. Myers created a complicated, heavy machine called an "Automatic Booth" in the late 1800s. It would be used in elections until 1980, at which point it was replaced by computers.

Did You Know?

Voters may mail in their ballots if they can't visit their polling places on Election Day. Members of the armed forces stationed away from home use this option. Absentee ballots date back to the Civil War!

Q Are state governments organized into branches like the federal government?

A Yes, each state has three branches to provide the same balance of power as the national government. The governor is the head of the executive branch, followed by the lieutenant governor. Voters elect these positions every four years along with things like a state attorney general and secretary of state. Each of the 50 states also has a legislative branch, made up of a state Congress, and a judicial branch that includes a state Supreme Court.

Q Do different offices serve different terms?

A Yes. A president or governor serves a term of four years. Members of the House of Representatives serve two-year terms, and senators serve six-year terms.

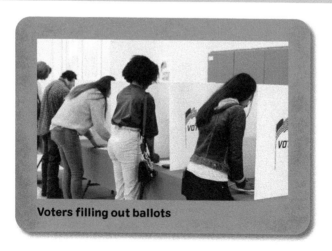
Voters filling out ballots

Q Does my city or town have a governor?

A No, the head of the local branch of government is called a mayor. Your town or city may also have a city council. Terms are commonly four years long.

Q What are some rules at polling places?

A Registered voters have to go to an assigned polling place based on their address. They may be required to bring a driver's license or other form of identification. Polling stations are required to accommodate voters with disabilities. Also, if voters are waiting in line when the polls close, they are allowed to cast their votes, no matter how long it takes.

Election official in Massachusetts

Did You Know?

The African country of Liberia has a similar government to the United States'. It has the same three branches of government and is considered a republic. The president serves a six-year term. Women have served in high-ranking positions in the government, including president.

Q Does Canada have the same type of government as the United States?

A They're neighbors, but they use different forms of government. Canada is a constitutional monarchy, which means that they recognize a king or queen as their head of state, but this is mostly a symbolic role, not a political one. Citizens can vote for members of Parliament, the House of Commons, and the Senate. The head of the government is called a prime minister.

Q What is the government in Mexico like today?

A It is a republic. There is a constitution, which divides duties of the government into the same three branches as the United States. Unlike the United States, though, the Mexican president is given more power than the other branches. Lots of decisions are left up to state and local governments, which is also similar to the United States.

GLOSSARY

abolish: To end something

absolute monarchy: A system of government in which one individual, usually a king or queen, makes all rules and laws

amendment: A change to an official document added after it's published

checks and balances: A method of preventing any one branch of government from having too much power

civil rights: Basic rights to be treated fairly and equally that every person has under the laws of the government

colony: Land that a far-away country claims as its own

constitution: A written document outlining a plan for government

constitutional monarchy: A form of government in which the power of the monarch is limited by a constitution

direct democracy: A form of democracy in which citizens can vote on each and every law in their country

executive branch: The government branch that carries out the laws, typically headed by a president

feudalism: A political system in which a king gives people land in return for services such as farming and military assistance

Founding Fathers: The group of people who set up the government of the United States of America

Indigenous: Native to a certain area

indirect democracy: A form of democracy in which citizens vote for officials to represent them, also known as representative democracy

judicial branch: The government branch, typically led by a Supreme Court, that makes sure laws are followed

legislation: Another word for a law or act passed by the government

legislative branch: The government branch that makes the laws; an example would be Congress

oligarchy: A type of government in which only a few people are in power

parliamentary government: A system of government in which a group of leaders pass the laws

popular vote: The overall vote of the citizens of the country

primary elections: The first round of presidential elections in which each political party selects its candidates

ratified: Voted on at the state level and passed, part of process of amending the Constitution

Reconstruction: The time period following the Civil War in the United States

republic: A type of government with an elected official in charge instead of a king or queen who inherits power

segregation: A system of being separated or kept apart, usually based on race

sovereign: The ultimate power or final word in a society

suffrage: The right to vote

theocracy: A system of government ruled by a religious figure

RESOURCES

Want to check out other resources so you can become more of a voting VIP and election expert? Here is a list of cool links you can visit to learn more about forms of government, the U.S. Constitution, the women's suffrage movement, and the accomplishments of presidents who made real change for voting rights.

Explore the U.S. Constitution.
constitutioncenter.org/interactive-constitution

Learn about influential American women.
womenshistory.org/resource-library-and-archives

Virtually visit library collections for past
U.S. presidents.
archives.gov/presidential-libraries

Learn more about the Magna Carta and the history of British politics.
britishmuseum.org

What about places to visit? Here is a list of sites to go to in person to learn more.

The Parthenon in Nashville, Tennessee, is a replica of a building in ancient Greece. No passport needed!
nashvilleparthenon.com

The National Archives building in Washington, D.C., houses important documents.
archives.gov

Visit the Smithsonian National Museum of African American History & Culture to explore civil rights issues and more.
nmaahc.si.edu

Head to Independence Hall in Philadelphia, Pennsylvania, to visit the spot where the Declaration of Independence was signed.
nps.gov/inde/planyourvisit/independencehall.htm

Printed in the USA
CPSIA information can be obtained
at www.ICGtesting.com
LVHW080957080124
768095LV00002B/3

9 798886 085624